CONTENTS

CHAPTER 1

FASHION
Designers

A model in a beautiful dress walks on a **catwalk**. Spotlights shine on her. Cameras take photos. People watching want to buy the dress.

BRIGHT IDEA BOOKS

YOU CAN WORK IN Fashion

by Samantha S. Bell

Raintree is an imprint of Capstone Global Library Limited, a company incorporated in England and Wales having its registered office at 264 Banbury Road, Oxford, OX2 7DY – Registered company number: 6695582

www.raintree.co.uk
myorders@raintree.co.uk

Text © Capstone Global Library Limited 2019
The moral rights of the proprietor have been asserted.

Edited by Charly Haley
Designed by Becky Daum
Production by Claire Vanden Branden
Originated by Capstone Global Library Ltd
Printed and bound in India

ISBN 978 1 4747 7531 1 (hardback)
22 21 20 19 18
10 9 8 7 6 5 4 3 2 1

ISBN 978 1 4747 7355 3 (paperback)
22 21 20 19 18
10 9 8 7 6 5 4 3 2 1

British Library Cataloguing in Publication Data
A full catalogue record for this book is available from the British Library.

Acknowledgements
We would like to thank the following for permission to reproduce photographs: iStockphoto: izusek, 18–19, Lise Gagne, 17, monkeybusinessimages, 25, PeopleImages, 22–23, powerofforever, 14–15, WinThom, 21; Shutterstock Images: Sarymsakov Andrey, cover (background), Anatolii Riepin, cover (foreground), iko, 6–7, lev radin, 13, magicinfoto, 5, Maria Moskvitsova, 28, Nata Sha, 26–27, ProStockStudio, 8–9, RazoomGame, 10–11, Sergei Domashenko, 31. Design Elements: iStockphoto, Red Line Editorial, and Shutterstock Images.

Every effort has been made to contact copyright holders of material reproduced in this book. Any omissions will be rec[...] [...]n given [...] [...] [...]lisher.

All the internet addr[...] [...] [...] at the time of [...]ing to press. However, due to the [...] of the internet, some addresses may have changed, or sites may have changed o[...] [...] since publication. While the author and [...]ublisher regret any inconvenience this m[...] [...] readers, no responsibility for any such change[...] [...]an be accepted by either the author or [...] [...]e publisher.

Someone designed the model's dress. Someone else made it. Other people will sell it. The people doing these things work in fashion.

A model walks down a catwalk in a fashion show.

A fashion designer
draws new clothing
ideas on paper.

All new clothes start with a design. A design shows what the clothes will look like. Fashion designers make the designs.

Designers draw their designs on paper. Sometimes they use a computer. They try to think of new ideas.

A fashion designer chooses the perfect fabric for each piece of clothing.

8

Designers choose **fabric** for the clothes. They think about how the fabric looks and feels. They decide how to put it together. They want the clothes to look good.

A fashion designer creates many different styles.

Some designers create **unique** clothes for famous people. Movie stars might wear that clothing. Other designers create clothes for shops. Lots of people wear that clothing.

Many fashion designers went to university. They studied design. Some start working as **interns** while they are at university.

FASHION CITIES

Some cities are famous for fashion, such as London, Paris and New York.

CHAPTER 2

FASHION
Models

Models wear new clothes. They help show new designs.

Some models are in fashion shows. They walk on catwalks. Many people watch to see the new clothes.

SUPERMODELS

Supermodels are models who earn a lot of money. They often become famous.

A model walks along the catwalk in a way that matches the clothing she is showing.

A photographer may tell a model how to pose.

Other models pose for photos.

The photos may be in magazines or catalogues. They may be online.

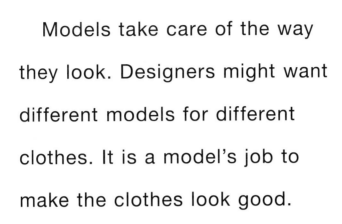

Models take care of the way they look. Designers might want different models for different clothes. It is a model's job to make the clothes look good.

Models usually have **agents**. Agents find jobs for models.

Sometimes models have a lot of work. They may travel a lot. At other times they just wait for the next job.

CHAPTER 3

PRODUCTION
Managers

Production managers decide how clothes will be made. They try to make **quality** clothing. They do not want to spend too much money.

The manager chooses a factory to make the clothes. The factory could be anywhere in the world. Managers may have to travel. Some managers want to help the environment. They try to make clothes without wasting **materials**.

A production manager works with other people.

17

A production manager may hold meetings to help work get done on time.

Managers must be organized. They must be good at working with people, too. They fix problems. They often work many hours in a day.

Most managers went to university. They may have studied business. Some managers have studied fashion.

CHAPTER 4

BUYERS

Buyers work for clothes shops. They choose the clothes the shops will sell.

Buyers go to trade shows to see new styles. They think about how well the clothes are made. They think about the price.

A buyer thinks about the quality of clothing.

Buyers plan ahead. They study fashion **trends**. They try to predict what customers will buy.

Some buyers may have a business degree.

A buyer tracks fashion trends.

Buyers also need work experience. Some start as a buyer's assistant. Some start by working in a clothes shop. They may start out as salespeople or **cashiers**. They may start as shop managers.

CHAPTER 5

FASHION
Journalists

Fashion journalists are writers. They report on fashion news.

Some fashion journalists write for magazines or newspapers. Others write for websites. Some attend fashion shows or parties. But they are there to work.

Journalists spend a lot of time at the computer. They write articles. They talk to fashion experts.

Journalists must be good writers. Many go to university. Some start working as interns. Others start by writing **blogs**.

A fashion journalist has to meet strict deadlines.

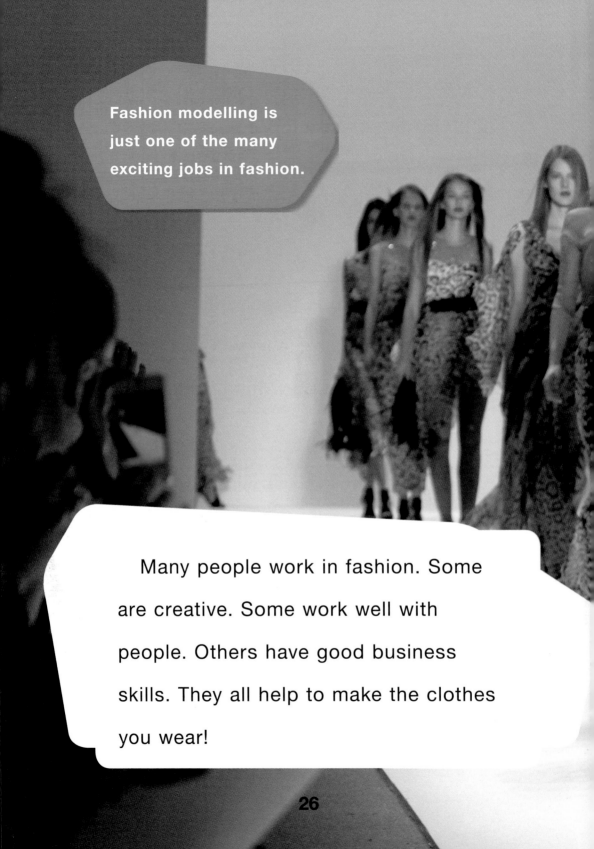

Fashion modelling is just one of the many exciting jobs in fashion.

Many people work in fashion. Some are creative. Some work well with people. Others have good business skills. They all help to make the clothes you wear!

GLOSSARY

agent
person who represents another person in business

blog
website where a person writes about personal experiences and opinions

cashier
shop worker who handles the money when customers buy something

catwalk
long stage that fashion models walk along to show clothes

fabric
cloth

intern
person who works without pay at a job for a certain amount of time to get experience

material
substance from which something is made

quality
level of value

trend
something that is currently fashionable or popular

unique
one of a kind

FIND OUT MORE

Want to know more about fashion? Check out these resources:

Books

Fashion: The History of Clothes, Jacqueline Morley (Book House, 2015)

How to Be a Fashion Designer, Lesley Ware (Dorling Kindersley, 2018)

Website

nationalcareersservice.direct.gov.uk/job-profiles/performing-arts-broadcast-and-media
This website tells you about jobs in fashion. Ask an adult or use a dictionary to help you understand any difficult words.

Places to visit

Fashion Museum, Bath
www.fashionmuseum.co.uk
See today's fashions and clothes from the past at this museum.

Victoria and Albert Museum, London
www.vam.ac.uk/collections/fashion
This museum has one of the largest fashion collections in the world.

ACTIVITY

DESIGN YOUR OWN CLOTHING FASHIONS!

All you need is some paper and a pencil. You can draw in a sketchbook or notebook. Then all your drawings will be in one place.

First, decide what kind of outfits you want to draw. You can draw something formal and beautiful. Try drawing a sports kit. Draw something casual. Remember to add shoes and accessories. You can colour in your drawings with felt-tip pens or coloured pencils.

INDEX